talkin basie

talkin basie

poems by
don kerr

cormorant books

Published with the assistance of The Canada Council, the
Ontario Arts Council, and the Saskatchewan Arts Board.

Cover by BearBrook Advertising.

Some of these poems appeared in *This Magazine* and some
were featured on CBC State of the Arts.

The section "Talkin Basie" is based on *Good Morning
Blues, The Autobiography of Count Basie*, as told to Albert
Murray, Random House, 1985.

The section "Solos" is based on *The World of Count Basie*,
Stanley Dance, Da Capo, originally published 1980.

The poem "Kansas City" is based on *Goin' to Kansas City*,
Nathan W. Pearson, Jr., University of Illinois Press, 1987.

The record I played fifty times a year as a teenager was
'Basie's Best', a 10 inch LP from Brunswick, BL5801,
with 'Every Tub', 'Sent for You Yesterday and Here You
Come Today' and 'Shorty George' on Side One. Can there
be greater pleasures.

Printed and bound in Canada.

Canadian Cataloguing in Publication Data

    Kerr, Don
    Talkin Basie

ISBN 0-920953-31-X

    I. Title.

PS8571.E71T34 1990   C811'.54   C90-090147-0
PR9199.3.K47T34 1990

*To David, Robert, William
and the pleasures of jazz*

Table of Contents

I home town
  10 home town
  11 bootleg jazz
  12 the dancing soprano
  14 Admission, Swing Has Its Value
  15 jazz is
  16 Benny
  17 doctor jazz
  18 the politics of jazz
  19 the organizer of silence
  20 radio waves

II Talkin Basie
  22 Talkin Basie
  36 Solos

III Kansas City
  52 Kansas City

IV Last of the Blue Devils
  58 rhythm method
  59 jazz weeds
  60 swing time
  61 Basie you never mentioned
  62 Last of the Blue Devils, Kansas City Reunion

V small heavens of jazz
  66 the MJQ
  68 dizzy red
  69 abdullah ibrahim
  71 the small heavens of jazz
  72 somebody came first
  73 hot vs. cool
  75 satin doll
  76 lady sundown
  77 Buddy Anderson says
  78 transport cafe
  81 UFO Blues, Gatemouth Brown
  86 round midnight

I   home town

home town

this country is country and western
this town's a farmers' town
mild mannered and built close to the ground
this town sings
weiner roast songs in the evening
and God Save the King in the morning
in this town the alto saxaphone
plays with fiddles and accordions
and people voted temperance ten to one
this house likes Bing Crosby
Bob Hope and Fibber McGee and Molly
this boy listens to the hit parade
and leaves the Sunday supper
to hide with his radio keeping score
of Theresa Brewer and the Mills Brothers
then one tall clear night the radio dial strayed
in this house and this boy discovered
New Orleans took the A Train to Harlem
been goin there ever since
first stop KC and the Count
One O'Clock Jump and Every Tub
and all the magic names and places

I had a dream and Kansas City
was its name

bootleg jazz

midway between
Moose Jaw and Prince Albert
stands New Orleans
I won my independence in New Orleans

in the wee small hours of the night
the band of light played every dream
I'd never known
Mr. Philco is the way and the light

bootleg jazz slips over the border
in the rumble seat
evading all customs

like
my mom and dad
and the CBC and Mario Lanzo
and Aunt Lorraine and scalloped potatoes

the Count and his men ran a flagwaver
all over town I never heard
anything like it
liner notes are my true delight
Down Beat is my bible
five stars on the page
beat five in the sky
hands down any old day

the dancing soprano

soprano life is the better life
we were told over sherry
a tone above flesh tone
a way to declare
the something better than
the places we were born

at the monthly letters' club
we paid we desperately paid
attention
to the music of
the delicate soprano
it said
read gibbon's history
and the odes of pindar
under ripples of piano
we shifted our low selves
on the straight-back chairs
while round us the elders
with sympathy and care
conducted the laboratory

could they exalt the low
transform the curling rink
into a concert hall
make the lilies of the field
sing soprano
monthly we held out our arms
for transfusions of sherry
could we by osmosis gain culture

but always like water
found our level after
harvesting beer
in the beverage room

where we paid
no attention at all
when the jazzband played
but danced happy to touch
in so many spots
members of the opposite sex

yet my partner of long standing
is none other than
the dancing soprano

the sherry's next the Duke and Count
and listens when the jazzband plays
what could be more rich
a lifetime filled with
dialectic

Admission, Swing Has Its Value

Arthur Collingwood, Dean of Music,
University of Saskatchewan, confessed today
that he had changed his point of view
on Tin Pan Alley and swing music.
'Through listening to the derangements
of fine tunes by slick technicians
students find their way back to the original
symphonic music. It is another case of
out of evil cometh good,'
he said.
'I've had repeated demands for the
B Flat Minor Concerto by Tchaikovsky.
They all prefer the original.'

Tchaikovsky's Piano Concerto was recorded
Feb. 25, 1942 by Glenn Miller and the deranger
was Bill Finegan. Dean Collingwood shoulda
flipped to Dipper Mouth Blues where Miller plays
the notes King Oliver charmed the snakes with
on the flip side of the garden of eden

jazz is in Saskatoon
relegated to the depths
a matter in the dark
whose name was
in the 40s and 50s the Cave
the Cavern and the Club 400
home of the mickey of rye
couples nosing forward
mapping out the dark
Fletcher Henderson played there
and Earl Hines Charlie Barnet
Eddie Durham and his all star girl band
starring Lips Hackette and the
Four Durhamettes

jazz is

jazz is in the summer of 36
in the *Queen's*
                    Quarterly

          a leery hooting
          couples grinding groins
          and grinding faces

I born that same hottest driest
summer of the great depression Basie
on the rise
               in far off Kansas City
while in Kingston Ont. Robert Nichols knows
his jazz by the book

          red carpet in the half dark
          where candles   .

                         guttered
          about a jazz band's

                         leery hooting
          a negro   who is bronzen
          with   gilded hair   beyond
          the grinding groins
the cathedral lifted silvering softly
beyond that local body house
where late the jazz band played

vengeance is mine saith the maker
of the home brew whose still
blew up in the basement of the
United Church during service
at the same historical time
or so it was written

Benny

hey now you watch that Benny Griggs
pitchin for Delisle walk up that mound
real slow like nobody
at Cairns Field would watch anybody
but Benny as if Benny
would watch nobody but Benny
do that lazy blue strut stretch
pause to check first the house
coil   smoke in a solo
Benny the walkin bass
pitchin trumpets burnt the burning
prairie air
gotta see yr first black man somewhere
he could make strikin out look more important
than a local guy doublin off the wall in centre

doctor jazz

hey man it's backbone music
guitar man plucks yr spinal cord
when he does the spinal cord blues
and he's way down
inside ya

works the other way round too
you got yr own life right
house job sidewalk wife well
you can walk right out
into that music man
go awol in that jungle

or to another planet that has got
absolutely nothin in common
with this one
all smoke and lights
spaced out man

buy yr ticket at the station
for the American Express
don't leave town without it
20th Century Unlimited
hey I got the spinal bluegitus
comatose until the blues
break it loose and I'm shakin
I'm shakin I'm shakin hey it's
okay I'm subsidin I'm
take it easy I'm
gonna be okay I'm
shakin
down
easy
yeh
okay
yeh

the politics of jazz

I been invaded by a foreign band
it captured my midsection
and it's workin both ways
it took over my feet
and it captured my head
I'm a jazz colony

the trouble with long hairs
he says now he's a jazz pod
is you can't talk
you can't drink
you can't dance
you can't tap
you can't hum
you just sit on a chair
and listen to those guys
who've memorized some other guy's stuff
who's been dead for years

I like a cat man not a copy cat
now jazz is
school lettin out yknow
or like all the desks in a row
should get up and move where they want
each day or just walk out

or it's a semi truck
running right over the people it loves
when the Base is in gear
man you don't just sit there
when the whole ocean's
about to roll right over you
you move
I feel an in
surrection comin on

18

the organizer of silence

there's all this silence
you gotta organize
chop it down with yr
sax and yr trumpet
and build it up again
they ask you
what you do for a livin
you tell em hey man
I'm the organizer of silence

radio waves

Ladies and Gentlemen
welcome to the Daisy Chain
in downtown Pittsburg
and those royal aristocrats of swing
Count Basie and his Band.
      a little Moten Swing signature
The boys are chomping on their instruments
so let's let them loose on the King Porter Stomp.
      short courtly stomp from King to Count
Now they slow down to 60 miles an hour
and present I'll Always Be In Love With You.
      piano piano piano
      hey Count, mercy mercy
      hey hey hey, count em out
      Count's on third
      and it's the hearta the batting order
      clayton young riff evans riff wells
      mercy
And now an instrumental and vocal dressing down
by James Rushing You Do the Darndest Things Baby.
      start high on the keyboard
      and work your way down
          you fly so high
          you do for a fall
All you swingology students rise and join
Swingtime at the Daisy Chain.
      it do move move move man
      mutedly trumpet modestly prez
      reed bed and brass walk
      natural born green guitar
      an old page walkin bass
      trumpet quiet whiskey neat
      trumpet sweet sundown hour
      fast but laid back
      goin places with style
February 10, 1937,
earliest surviving Basie broadcast,
last recording session, December, 1983.

20

II   Talkin Basie

Talkin Basie

1.

I woke up one morning in Tulsa
about eleven hot muggy and
hungover in the Red Wing Hotel
and I heard that music
figured it must be a record of Louis
but it was the Blue Devils
doin a ballyhoo and I'd never
heard a band like that
havin such a good time
Walter Page and the Blue Devils
and that was Hot Lips Page blowin
first time I heard Rush sing
washed the booze
right outa my head
first time I knew
just what I wanted to do

good morning blues

Henry Murphy set me to playin
upstairs on Deep Second Street
I'd play just before suppertime
and when the good corn liquor came out
so I was covered for food and juice
knew all the joints to go to
that was Oklahoma City
Blue Devils came to town
for a breakfast dance at Slaughter's Hall
piano player took sick and I sat in
there was no sheet music
someone would call out a tune
and away they'd go

later I got a telegram from Paris
Paris Texas   come join the Blue Devils
they were a commonwealth band
everybody got the same money
if you had a family you got a bit more

Rush and me would hit the alley joints
after hours me playing piano him singin
find those nice ladies
find somethin to eat and drink
never got rich
hell I had to buy a four dollar hat
on time

2.

learned piano from Miss Vandervere
at 25¢ a lesson in Red Bank New Jersey
and I could pick out any tune I heard
ragtime was big back then
I was in short pants but I was mannish
wantin to be on my way

bought a monkey-back suit
and in 1924 went to New York
got a road job with a burlesque show
rode the Pullman to all those cities
Dayton Indianapolis Toledo Chicago
playing for a sepia dance act
and staying out of lily white hotels

3.

this time in Kansas City
I stayed at the Booker T Washington Hotel
across 18th from the Eblon on the mainstem
a few steps down was Jones Pool Hall
the Lincoln Dance Hall and the barbershop
the Subway Club was at 18th and Vine
Piney Brown's at 18th and Highland
Streets Hotel at the corner of 18th and Pascoe
Yellow Front Saloon at 18th and Lydia
on Independence Avenue Big Joe Turner
was the singing bartender
serving whiskey by the dipper
Mary Lou Williams played the Lincoln
and I got outa her way cause she
was tearin everybody up
heard the territory bands
heard Fletcher Henderson heard Andy Kirk
and his Twelve Clouds of Joy

Hey said Fletch come on up and play this
but it had too many sharps
I wasn't gonna mess around with all them sharps
I wasn't gonna sit in with Fletch
they did stuff in hard keys
I wasn't gonna get stuck up there
in a hard key

4.

Moten's was a commonwealth band
and they had a meeting
and voted the leader out
voted Bennie Moten out of
the Bennie Moten orchestra
and voted me in as leader
I had no idea when I went in that room
and there it was
Count Basie and his Cherry Blossom Orchestra
I'd named myself Count earlier
but nobody paid attention
my buddy Eddie Durham says
when we arranged together
and I'd give an idea and skip out
while he wrote it and get a drink
and he'd say where's that no count rascal

that band broke up pretty soon
and Jo Jones and I hung around
in Little Rock getting raggedy ass poor
Bennie organized another band
and asked me to join a prince of a man
when were on the road he died you know
under the knife in a small operation
I'm not even going to try to say
all the things he meant to me

5.

got me a pontiac
roadster with a rumble seat
60 miles an hour
Moten Swing
and a wife about the same time
car worked better than the marriage
everybody was doin it
gettin a car and a wife
couldn't find our way outa Philadelphia
with that car went round and round
left it at a garage and took the bus to Baltimore
last time I saw that car
finance people musta found it
can't remember when Vivian left

gonna help myself to a bite from this guy's plate
and he says every tub base every tub
meanin every tub's got its own bottom
ain't nobody here gonna feed you
look out for yourself man
I fill up a full plate a grub
hey base he says every tub man every tub

6.

someplace in Ohio we stopped over
and went into a bar for a sandwich
and they had a piano in there
it wasn't bothering anyone
but I went over and started to bother it
don't know why I hopped on that innocent piano
probably good looking girls in the place
but that was Art Tatum's piano
and they went and got him
just waiting for someone to mess with his piano
and he's a keyboard monster
so I won't forget that
one of the girls at the bar said
I coulda told ya. Why didn't you baby,
I asked, why didn't you?

I remember walking downstairs one night
when Duke had this thing going
I got halfway down and all that music hit me
I had to turn around and get another drink
and then come back down
one step at a time
I just had to get myself together
to face all that

had to play each night with that monster
Oscar Peterson and he'd play a chorus
and I'd stumble through one and he'd help me
or forget me and I'd have to hit those keys hard
to let him know I was still alive
I'd think of that monster
and my whole day was ruined
how can anybody think and play that fast?
he just puts his hands out and they play
I wait in the wings with a baseball bat

7.

all the time I'd been in Kansas City
I never went downtown
all I ever needed was on 12th and 18th
never went below Troost
then I went to the Reno
and got their band
and the guys came in
from the old Blue Devils
one by one and from Moten's band
and that was the real beginning

we were at the Reno in 1937
Count Basie and his Orchestra
radio station came down a couple of times a week
and broadcast an hour S9XBY
we never thought much about it
but a lot a people heard us
Lester Young heard us and come to join
and John Hammond heard us
and wanted us to record
sometimes we ran outa tunes
and I'd just start somethin
and give it a title
so one night we'd run out and the announcer asked
what's the name of this one and I looked at the clock
and said One O'clock Jump and we hit it with the rhythm
section
and went into the riffs and the riffs just stuck
started in D flat and went on in F
played all the flagwavers we could
and set the two tenor men to battle
Herschel and Lester and I'd tell em things
to fire em up about the other
folks would come round the bandstand
and cheer for one or the other

signed my first record contract with Decca
$750 a year   no royalties   for 24 sides a year
$31 a song   I guess they cheated us
John Hammond was mad when he heard about it
and got the boys scale

8.

I knew what that band should sound like
what each section and each guy
should sound like
back when I dictated arrangements to Eddie Durham
I could actually hear the band playing those passages
while we worked on them

the guys always knew when to come in
and once they'd played something
they could damn near play it the same
next night I'd say things like
take it down, half a tone and
go for something
there was a leader in each section
two or three years we did those head arrangements
Jumping at the Woodside
Shorty George
Every Tub

9.

we went the southern route
hitting Fort Worth   San Antonio   Galveston
Houston   Henderson and Port Arthur and then
Baton Rouge   New Orleans and Monroe
then we swung up to Little Rock
came back down to Birmingham
crossed over to Atlanta
dipped down to Jacksonville
and headed north by way of
Macon Knoxville Louisville and Bowling Green
one nighters and people had heard the records
and the radio shows and asked for their favorites
One O'Clock Jump   Dickey's Dream   Lester Leaps In
Blue and Sentimental   Shorty George
Sent For You Yesterday   Goin to Chicago

Count Basie's book on tour
down highway #13   Camrose   Bawlff
Daysland   Strom   Killam
playing words all the way
Lougheed   Hardisty   Amisk   Czar
rain clouds boiling all down that sky
Alberta Pool takes a tall green solo

by the time brother Dicky
hooked up with us
he'd been with Charlie Johnson
Fletcher Benny Carter Teddy Hill
Wendel had been with Billy Eckstein
Earl Hines and Benny Carter
and also with the Benny Goodman sextet
Jimmy had been a high note man
in Lionel Hampton's great band
also with Charlie Barnet and Lucky Millinder

10.

after Pearl Harbour guys were concerned
cause a bunch of them were 1A
I said I wasn't goin anyplace
I ain't gonna take that trainin
goin out on manoeuvers
jumpin in foxholes
with them goddamn snakes
and things
out there in the swamp
nothin they could do to me
as bad as what them snakes
would make me do to myself

11.

things were drying up for the big band by 1950
be bop and I don't know what all
the only ones left from the old Reno days
were Jimmy Rushing and Jack Washington
from the Famous Door times there was
Freddie Green Earle Warren Sweets and Dickie Wells
I got tired of being out on the road
catch as catch can and I just said that's it
that was the end of the band
I brought out from Reno City

after a while I needed money
and started up a sextet
with Clark Terry and Buddy de Franco
and when we got back to New York
Freddie Green turned up with his guitar
and I said what the hell you doin here?
and he looks at me or the wall
or out in space and says
you're workin tonight aren't you?
and that was it
we became a septet
and he's been there ever since

European audiences were great
I hated flying so I got a little help
from Mr. Scotch and Mr. Bourbon
but not enough
1954 landed in Copenhagen
and finally got to Paris France
and not just Paris Texas
had such a good time
I honestly didn't know where I was half the time

I didn't get a look at the city
the city got a look at us
when we played Royal Festive Hall
in London we turned up without the music
and the guys played by memory
that audience was so quiet
no buzzing no room noise just
listening and applauding
Princess Margaret came
and sat through two shows
met the Queen and you can't beat that
in Great Britain

that was on the sixth trip to England
but after awhile all those towns
run together
and then we and then we
yeh
and in Japan we played Mito Tokyo
Sapporo Kanazawa Nagoya and and
yeh
it's in the scrapbook

Solos

12.

Jimmy Rushing Sings

My daddy gave me a violin
and locked up the piano and said
if I ever catch you on that piano again
or dancing I'm gonna
but mother gave me the key
when I moved out I found the blues
were everywhere
I was just a beginner
a three key piano player
so they told me I better sing
there were no microphones back then
you had to hold your own
to overshadow those horns
I had a big pair of lungs

everybody got the same every night
$1.36 or $7.10 and we were happy
if we had a bad night we were told
go grab your girls and if they liked you
they'd feed you and give you a bit of money
never went to a party unless we could all go
there was a certain amount of brotherly love
in those days but not anymore

13.

Trumpet Solo by Buck Clayton

I learned piano in my home town
Parsons Kansas
my father was a minister
sang in a church choir with Wild Bill Davis father
listened to Coon Saunders on the wireless
Bennie Moten came through town
I organized a six piece band when I was twelve
but people were down on jazz
guys got killed at a dive called the Bucket of Blood
and at the Yellow Frontier in Kansas City
my mother thought it was finally okay
when we played Carnegie Hall in 38

there's no drinking in Carnegie Hall

someone taught me scales on the trumpet
that was all   first job I had I only knew one song
Dinah   and played it all night long for five dollars
but pretty soon I was arranging cause I'd had piano
and a guy showed me this is trombone this is trumpet

I had my own band when I was 21
and we went to Shanghai and played two years
didn't want to learn Chinese
too many dialects
be like learning English in New York City
and then going to Newark
they wouldn't know what you were talking about
tried to get the band to go to New York
but western guys like their barbecue pits
the way New York boys like their after hour spots
I stopped off on the way to New York to see my mother
and joined Basie when Lips Page quit
I don't think I was good enough then
to follow Lips

I was there seven years before I went into the army
I was luckier than Lester
they shipped him to Alabama
but they needed a trumpet player
and I got in the band

14.

Drum Solo by Jo Jones

in my formative years
I didn't always know where I was
I didn't major in geography
all I knew is I was travelling
and I had aunts and uncles
everywhere in show business
to teach me   come on kid siddown
and watch this

in the 20s and 30s you did what you were told
those were the social conditions in those times
Mr. Earl Hines had to play with a knife at his throat
in Chicago   a lot of great players just quit
because they couldn't do what they wanted
became winos or worked in packing houses
or running an elevator

I first played with Basie in Topeka
but after I heard Lester on After You've Gone
I cut out   I had to go back to school
but they kept me there   Joe Keyes sat by me
and taught me how to think
they had no music
they just called a tune and played

when it comes to musical wealth
I'm the richest drummer that ever lived
look at those guys up front every night
never will be an institution
like the Basie band when it started
we were behind the Iron Curtain too
Kansas City had to play for ourselves
we were thinking nothing but music

15.

Arrangement by Eddie Durham

formed a family band just after the war
my cousin Herschel Evans was in it
that was in San Marcos Texas
I played banjo four string guitar
trombone six string guitar

I added the sixth and ninth chords
with Moten so we did five part harmony
with the brass and that was okay
because everyone was playing their own note
before that they'd say hey you playin my note
get off my note

Walter Page changed the sousaphone
into the bass fiddle and he was so strong
you could hear that bass fiddle walk
I put a resonator on a string guitar
you hit it near the mike and it sounded electric

Moten was out of songs so I took a show off
wrote Moten Swing with Basie
and they ran through it played it next night
and the people went crazy

you know everybody was playing as much piano
as they could and along comes Basie who plays
as little as he can
got a girls band together in the war
only way I could stay out of the army
play bond drives did 4000 miles
in Canada for the Canadian government

16.

Alto Bridge by Earle Warren

when I joined Basie I swear to God
I had cold chills   I had never
heard anything like Prez
he knew changes like nobody's business
he'd turn his horn up in the air
like he was smoking a pipe

had a softball team
Prez pitched I was shortstop
Herschel first base   Jack Washington
on second   Edison in short centre

I got all the bridges
eight bars in the middle of everything
when I went with Basie
I was making $6.25 a night
the nights we were working

we played two baritones two tenors
to get a deep dark sound for ballads

17.

Trombone Solo by Dicky Wells

I sat in and said where's my music
sit down said Basie and start fannin
Basie would vamp a little
set a tempo
set a rhythm for the saxes
and Earle Warren would pick it up and lead the saxes
then one for the bones
now it's our rhythm against theirs
next the trumpets would start fannin
with their derbies
solos would fall in between ensembles
it was a big band
but he handled it like six pieces
my six weeks with Basie turned into eleven years

only new thing the band had
was the battle of the tenors
Prez and Herschel two of the best
Herschel Buddy and Illinois all came from Texas
so they have that big Texas sound

I'd take an arrangement in
and Basie would say
that's enough for fifty arrangements
and whittle it down
keep only a bit
but it swung

Prez made up the names
Harry Edison was Sweets
Basie The Holy Main
Buck Clayton Cat Eye
Ed Lewis Big Doc
Benny Morton was Mr. Bones and when Benny left
I became Mr. Bones
Freddie Green was Pep
Walter page the Big Un
Herschel Evans Tex
Earle Warren Smiley
Jo Jones Sampson
and so on

some bands sound too perfect
doin everything precise
but you've lost the fun
kids playin in the mud
and a mother calls one to clean up
so he cleans up and looks real good
but he can't have fun no more

18.

Trumpet Solo by Harry Edison

one of my glorious moments came
after I joined Basie in 38
and we played Owensboro
and my aunt and uncle came in a horse and buggy
and he was so proud
he told everybody   I taught him
what he's doin today   I taught him

came home from school one afternoon
and here was Lips Page next door
talking to this beautiful girl
musicians were getting all the girls
he accomplished overnight
what I'd been trying to accomplish for four years
that's when I decided to become a trumpet player

we couldn't wait to get on the bandstand
like a horse prancing to get on the track

Basie noodles around till he gets it right
like mixing mash and yeast to make whiskey
and you keep tasting and tasting
Freddie Green and Jo Jones would follow
till he hit the right tempo and they'd hold it
that rhythm section would send chills up my spine
every night
that's the greatest band that's ever
been on earth
I was with him from 38 to 50
but I still go back to him

he liked everybody in that band
but it was Lester Young's playing
that he loved

44

19.

Tenor Solo by Buddy Tate

a lot of tenor players wanted to go with Basie
they called me because of a jam I'd had with Prez
five or six years before
Skippy Williams was there   he wanted the gig
second night we played a white college dance
and the kids kept asking for Blue and Sentimental
Herschel's showcase and Basie looked down and said
you know that?   I can try I said   E flat Basie said
I'd never played it   I'd listened to the record a lot
everybody danced and it broke up the house
and the band stood up and shook my hand
I had a job

in 43 they fired Don Byas   know why?
Ben Webster came down one night
and played in Don's chair
I never heard anyone sound like that
Don went across the street and got stoned

the army finished Prez
he was a happy cat before that
they put him in the brig
for a long time

20.

Lockjaw Davis Solos on Scotch

I been in this business long enough
to endorse liquors the ones without the hangover
right now I'd like to endorse Cutty Sark
I could endorse cigarettes
I know the taste of cigarettes
we always play in dungeons full a smoke
some groups start the first set fine
and get ragged by the fifth set
you know why that is
they haven't programmed their drinking
I start on beer and end on Scotch and milk
I've taped my evenings on different combinations
so I know what to drink to play
it's scientific jazz

21.

Trumpet Solo by Joe Newman

had a family band in New Orleans
I was seven when I started playing cornet
I soloed at eight they stood me on a chair
Louis was my influence and then Roy
I had his picture on my door
from Louis came Roy from Roy came Dizzy

22.

Alto Bridge by Preston Love

The six weeks I spent in that band in 43
were utopian
I'd listened to those records thousands of times
I was 22 and spelling Earle Warren
I was so enthusiastic I became a kind of pet
when I heard Dickey Wells blowing those obligatos
behind me on Moten Swing
I could hardly restrain my emotions
I got back in 45 when Warren left again

It was a great thrill to play the Orpheum
in Omaha   to go from the poverty of Love's Mansion
and Omaha's ghetto to the Orpheum
it seemed too far fetched for a black kid of my generation

46 was the last glory year for the Basie band of the 30s and
40s
bebop was on the horizon and we hadn't had a hit
young guys told me at a concert
it was all over   Diz was where it's at
that old cat Tate has gotta go
tell Basie he's gotta move with the times
you're a young cat you know the score
bookings fell off and the calibre of places
and we had more and more unpaid vacations

23.

Alto Sax Solo by Bobby Plater

I joined in the 60s
I had visions of these guys getting together
and jamming but these guys never jam
they work hard and never have much time
but I still want to play
jamming is where the ideas are born
they're not born from a pen

III   Kansas City

Kansas City

Sure I'll tell you about Kansas City.
That was Boss Tom's town and it was
screamin lit up and wide open.
I didn't know what a politician was
but I learned fast enough
the machine was boss
and it was Tom's machine.
It was the depression everywhere else
but not in Kansas City
not in Tom Pendergast's town
cause he had a deal with the mafia
who had a deal with the police
and that's the truth.

I was young and it was a great town.
All you worried bout was a good time
who you gonna date tonight
where you gonna go
who you gonna jam with.
Oh it was joyous every night
it was joyous just thinkin
what you gonna do that night.

Prohibition was nothin absolutely
nothin in Kansas City
beer for a nickel whiskey for a dime.
But that corn whiskey was tough
and there were mean places.
Guys start shootin at one another
take a knife to one another.
One night I took my horn
and jumped right out the window
but they came and brought me back to play.

Sure there were plenty a gangsters in KC
but those guys were a musician's best friend
give you a job a bite to eat some juice a loan.
They looked after you.
They do their job we do ours.
Pretty Boy Floyd would come round
unlimber do the lindy hop
wonderful man the dude
saw him four days before he got killed
playin pool listenin to the bands
and the police came in and warned him
the feds was on their way.

Red light district was sure as hell
lit up and wide open
anything you could think of
chicks take dollar bills off a table edge
with those little old twats.
Well that's just what happened
I won't say no more

Some places were so full of marijuana
you'd get a buzz just sittin there.
Stuff grew along the highways in Nebraska
so we'd stop and cut it
look like a bale of hay
tie it on the car roof
speed up to dry it out.
When booze became legal
those gangsters started dealin drugs
and heroin oh that was Bird
broke every morning
hawking his horn.
A whole generation of cats was done in
on that stuff half of Jay McShann's first band
dead on that stuff in ten years
includin the Bird.

That town was wide open and lit up
twenty four hours a day
music twenty four hours a day
Yellow Front Saloon
the best night shift in town
spook breakfasts
people waitin at a street car stop
goin to work just drop in
drop their lunch buckets and stay all day
the blues comin outa windows and doors.
It might have been the depression someplace else
but not in Boss Tom's town
not in Kansas City.
Start at eight at the Reno and play till four
you want somethin you just get up and walk back
band keep on playin
never knew what Basie'd play next
start a riff and I'd lead
and the horns would follow.
Whites only on the dance floor
blacks in the balcony or behind the band.
At four go jammin at the Sunset
Big Joe Turner and Pete Johnson
doin a forty minute blues
makin it all up as they went along
words and all.
Had those gunfighter jam sessions
leave a note for a visitor
I'll be playin at the such and such
if you dare I'll see you there.
I'll bet there's more boys from Kansas City
than anyplace else can tell you how the day breaks.

Everybody came to Kansas City.
All over the world you'd hear about
18th and Vine.
You didn't make a lot of money
but everybody took care of everybody
and you had one helluva time.

And that was for twenty years and why hell for ten
Kansas City was the centre of the USA.
Look on any map.
But in '39 the feds caught Boss Tom for embezzling
to pay his gamblin debts and tax evasion
and sent him away
and there was the reformers
and a tax on dance halls
and a one o'clock curfew in Kansas City
can you believe it
then there was the war took a lot of guys
took Jay McShann right off the bandstand
and that was that for Kansas City.

IV   Last of the Blue Devils

rhythm method

Count Basie asked me to tea
Lady Day said come right in
Prez made the dressing
for a salad Dickie tossed
Buck barbecued ribs
those KC ribs and Jimmy
sang for our supper
I was friends of them all
I spent a lot of time there
in the basement
of the mansion on the hill
never told my family though
about those low down times
but I was a good listener
so I heard it all
that riffin ready talk
and who kept horning in
and makin no bones about it
their base habits
sax in the afternoon
and in the nighttime too
a reed you can lean on man
the tenor of their talk
horn a plenty
ribs and whiskey
and the black and white
yeh black and white
keys to it all
loved those low down bones
some barbecue and sweet licks
no strings attached
just plain all out
brass attacks blue thunder
and that old tried and true
rhythm method

jazz weeds

jazz weeds
growin up round
my back door
across the track music
race records
and I don't mean ben johnson
gutbucket bloodbucket whiskey still music
funky mojo barbecue jazz
and the last shall be first
King Huckleberry and Duke Jim
shacktown royalty
screendoor living
and the sun that shines
shines all over town
where the Count walks and the Duke walks
and King Oliver and the Earl of Hines
where President Young and Sir Charles Thompson
walks in that same sun as Mr. Pendergast
the boss of KC and his protege
Mr. Truman prez of the cold war
and the hot bomb you want
hot and cool that don't hurt
go back down to the peeled
side a town for warm buck
cool prez warm ribs
and cold chicken warm whiskey
and cold beer warm women
and cool evenings
back down where the jazz weeds
grow up round
my back door
and sin
stays home

swing time

we put the band in jail
cause they was speedin
we put the one a clock jump
in their with em
that's too late man
we got a curfew
speedin on the airwaves
and stayin up late
and then disturbin the peace
just too loud the neighbors
was complainin
you feel you gotta do it do
an eight a clock jump
then we got em for runnin
through the end of the song
without stoppin three times
we got no complaints about the piano player
nice and quiet but he's the ringleader
okay says the judge sixty days
thirty days off for playing ballads
next case

Basie you never mentioned

Basie you never mentioned where I saw you
at some dance hall on Lake Ontario
with a blind date in 1959
and a guest appearance by Jimmy Rushing
we saw at George's in Toronto the next week
and he did all those blues
the same every night
like he was a 4 x 4 blues machine
every pound from another life
English graduate students
knew nothing of
high on Frye
groovin on McLuhan
beer we held in common
the girl I kissed goodnight to in Hamilton
had cold lips next to the heat
of trumpet by Buck or Sweets
I should have felt more than I did

I mean about the band

Last of the Blue Devils, Kansas City Reunion

I don't want no documentary
bout where jazz has been and gone
I don't want no rundown streets
no heroes playin in the legion hall
so shut yr eyes and let the blues
do the walkin and the talkin

cause everythin's gonna be alright

I don't want no documentary
I don't want to see no deli
where the jazz bands played
no bowlin alley and no dry cleaner
where the blues was sung

you so beautiful but you gotta die someday

I don't want no documentary
I don't want no 18th and vine
lookin like a dead end corner
I don't want no empty lot
let old Joe Turner sing
I was standin on 18th and vine
dreamin man dreamin of Piney Brown

with all the world dear at my command

I don't want no documentary
where the colour's gone to rot
and the guys can't talk
except with their mouths
and what they say is flat
and the sound is bad
let the blues walk and talk
get your camera outa Kansas City
and let the dance band roll

tain't nobody's business if I do

everythin's gonna be alright
commodore Count's layin it down
travellin to beat the band
cause somebody's organized
the mayhem man
Jay McShann's makin that piano march
makin that piano strut
riffin things up man

and the last word by the last
of the blue devils is
think about everybody boys
bout Count Basie and Jay McShann
Hot Lips Page and Big Un too
Jo Jones Joe Turner and Eddie Durham
think about everybody boys
but don't forget the little man
is the last word
last solo last blues of the last
of the Blue Devils.

V   small heavens of jazz

the MJQ

these four elegant gents
chord an obstacle
then play right through

featherin a nest of notes
left hand   right hand
                  fly away
                                                    fly away

land and

                s k i t t e r
abcabcabcabc
                  riff   riff   riff

and getaway to someplace
leave no trace
always in the best of taste

clark kent and the mild mannered quartet
fingers tickling the
                          skin of time

a rhythm where we've all been
who've any ear to town

the glass-clad-new-and-cool town
              over
music   the barcelona
        under_{chair}

keyboard buildings solo
in the sky high air
tasty waves breaking their

cool   little   curves
on that thin ribbed sand

clouds in the blue sky
hung out to dry
sun
    f i l t e r i n g

        through

up and down the glass facade
in and out the mezzanine

music to make
a spinach salad to

Ladies and Gents

    the MJQ

dizzy red

Gillespie's fulla brass
breakneck traffic on the interstate
whiskey music straight up
cadillac brass

8 mm brass
cuttin through
            latitudes and long held
                        customs

    Dizzy scattering seed
    at so many miles per hour
               on automatic
            with his chromatic
  set to red
        red fast and red
               s l o w
  a limited spectrum but
             hecticer
               and
             hecticer

street talk trumpet
bull fight trumpet
seed bag trumpet

        doing the clover leaf reds
        high thin and then some

  30 years later it's the same
  roar on the same number
  blazing red
  preserved in amber

abdullah ibrahim

finger on the pulse of

now   night   town   heart
and then

ideal melody
plays in the silence
in his head

appears from his finger tips
like coins
like scarves

what you hear are the notes
he chooses not
to play

they surround the notes
he does play

gently in clusters
or all alone   muted
fingers

melody's the town
you know your way round
improvise n yr out there
on yr own
life on the line
every time

his harlem   cape town   raized
music plays his way back
musicians are
says abdullah ibrahim
healers   making music
doctor jazz
with the late night
starside manner

the small heavens of jazz

radio played over and over
the small heavens of jazz
and the sun like a pale heart
in the skeleton trees beat mildly
an ocean arriving over and over
on the shore faintly like the bass
in the trio while the fingers of
hampton hawes turned the tumblers
and they all escaped
down the coastal highway
from the long arm
of the self

somebody came first

somebody came first
in each room
blew the first trumpet
notes somewhere in the stars now
played the first game of snooker
in the Westside Emporium
fathered the realtor who squared the city
even eternal righteousness
began somewhere
day and night go one way
on their super continental
you go another
upstream into antiques
searching the wooden stores for a record
Buddy Bolden made
or someone who remembers 1903
before the city came

hot vs. cool

fetched up on a ledge
on the hottest day of summer
an electric fan battled upriver
all
   the
       long night long

summer crawling in every pore
                    every crease
                    every minute
                    every
move all night
            lay
in the three room cave

                    dreaming
of cool
       iceberg clouds
       lakes of shade

       paul desmond   lightly

and am delighted to be unremittingly
hot and bothered
                    alto
                sultry now
in the airshaft
on the fire escape
all
   the
       long night long
            in the shadow
of the trumpet SUN

awash with   summer
                     pulp fiction

flesh a fountain on a slow burn

           joni mitchell airborne
             on a tall cool solo

satin doll

the cloud came over the hill
for a look the moon played
piano fingers rapidly spidering
in the far room over the finest contour
rising to the occasion a mouth full
of lies the room throbbing
like an ocean liner the moon
fingering the black keys
of the sea her inner landscape
plum full her breasts scented
trouble her clouds filling with breath
she sails out on a limb
moonlighting clouds tumble
pillows and black satin the alto
the tenor and the bass three minutes
of the best

lady sundown

The sun is setting.
How can I keep my hands off you.
The wind is mild.
Used car lots are in bloom.
Can I forgive your clothes?
The brandy is jumping
and the chevy's in gear.
Have a snifter of jazz.
An art disco sky.   Red lips
at the junction.   Neon lady.
Pastel scarves dropping away
one by one from the sky.
The next waltz is ours.

Buddy Anderson says

Bird and those cats made some awful mistakes.
They had a chance to take people with them
but they played for themselves.
They got too conscious about what they were doin.
Exhibitionism is what it was.
Everythin too damn fast or too damn slow
no middle tempo no dance tempo.
Then they quit singin.
Miles turned his back on people.
That's the sign how far they went.

This used to be street music
Cats don't go on the streets anymore.
They've become middle classish
gettin a little sterile.
They oughta go out there with the people
play what the people wanta hear.
We used to be where
everybody was.
Now we're out on the edge of things.
Replaced by rhythm and blues and rock and roll
out on the edge of things.
Those cats are famous cats
but they made some awful mistakes.

transport cafe

the chef said not to worry
we'd fetch up home at last
he grinned geared up
put his foot on the gas
and the long narrow cafe
began to shake and groan
hadn't been started for years
the double boiler shuddered
shot a fat arrow of steam
the chimney plumed black smoke
and the 18 wheeler cafe
rolled into the avenue
and the beautiful women
at the wafer tables looked round
astounded as if finally a day
just might live up to their
private dreams I ordered champagne
the drivers began to roll
the birds on the cornice
flew down in the street
we swung right to 20th
traffic looking so sad standing there
out of the picture
while the bistro went west
towards the great tableland of prairie
laid out in place settings long ago
I offered champagne to the next table
where the famous local artist
had begun already to draw
the rundown streets we journey through
and she said yes it's wonderful
meaning today and there was no
stopping us police cars howling
but scattered before the inevitable
ride of the diner serving now

soufflé and dry wine
the radio talked about us
as if we were another weather
disturbance while we
thought of ourselves as
music
each according to his taste
a piano appassionato lunching
on gazpacho a tenor sax
doing urban in country
a guitar making small classical
waves in the champagne
the sky filling and emptying
with clouds and the prairie
a patchwork of sunlake
would we ever stop
asked the beautiful ladies
in their nimbus of story
and I settled for
no ending at all
or ever returning
there was food enough
in the sweet cafe for days
and steam enough
to gain the next and the next
horizon and art enough to draw on
like a bank account
and no end in sight to
talking with beautiful ladies
or the towns that loved us
the neon cafe that rode the
outskirts of sundown
tv cameras followed us through
the night we the bright star
the most famous cafe

in the history of cafes
mountains begin to climb
at the back of our minds
the valley of the sun
the fruit hanging in clusters
the delta land green as fire
and the great plains of the sea
waving us in to berth

UFO Blues, Gatemouth Brown

1.

got a one track song
and we ain't comin back
cause this song runs
to the end of the track

boy waitin at the station
for the evenin special
ear to the track
hears them rails a hummin
gatemouth highballin
whistle whistle whistle
roar roar roar
and gone
them rails a hummin
in that boy's mind
for years

express train blowin
through town after town
gramma in her bedroom
looks out to see what the
what the what the
look out gramma
we're comin on through
roar's declared
farmer in his field grins on account
he took out his jazz insurance
let gatemouth huff and puff
flattenin grain with all that
blowin goin by farmer says oh yeh
gatemouth do your stuff

train firin down the line
set the snowfence alight
hey little black eyed susan
look way up this is yr day
cinders bouncin in the ditch
hot time in weed town tonight

quarter mile from that runaway train
the aspen leaves shiver
like spider fingers on that
piano man delicate in the eye a the
rhythm section man it
do go it do
go

and gone man gone really gone
see like it was howlin on down the grade
on the grand trunk line just west a purdue
and it kept on goin know what I mean
outa sight man straight up like I mean
inta the sky and they ain't been seen since
gone man gone

2.

so we're sitting around one night
mindin our own beeswax
havin a beer or two or three
shootin the breeze
and who should we hear
I mean right outa the blue
but gatemouth brown
and this is way out on the edge
a nothin and he's playin those UFO Blues
and we look way up and it's the
starlight express come steamin down
playin I been travellin man
to some way out places
past the twilight zone and the whiskey way
got lonesome and blue and spaced out too
got lonesome and blue so we cranked up that old bass fiddle
climbed aboard worked up a heada steam
and played ourselves right back home
far out man far out

and us guys were just sittin around
in the back of the gas station
in an old log cabin on the old
lonesome and long
land we love
know what I mean
and down come that whole band
watch those drummers roll
gatemouth brown with the throttle in his hand
come to tell us the news
where they been travellin to
singin I been everywhere man
and now I'm playin the UFO Blues
so they settled in on the single track
goin back east and they slowed down now nice and
slooww and we climbed aboard pickin up speed now

pickin up speed commencin to pick up speed
doin the UFO blues doin
have you heard the news
I got the UFO blues

well my baby kicked me out of our own place
said she had to find her own space
yeh yeh yeh her own space
so I figured what I had to do
was find a way to find my space too
well I went all the way out to outer space
spaced out man
and here's what I found out in outer space
farther you go the lonelier you get
and I went so far I'm lonely yet
farther you go the lonelier you get
and I went so far I'm lonely yet

baby take me back
I'm on a one way track
one way track
baby take me back
I got the UFO Blues
travellin on down that line
blowin those towns away
whistle plays alto
wheels play rhythm
and then gatemouth played
and then gatemouth played
and we listened
opened a beer or two or three
then they played

tell you the news
got the UFO Blues
got tired of star light star bright
baby comin home to you tonight
don't wanta be no UFO Blue
just wanta be in bed with you

and then they played
travellin east
travellin west
midnight rambler
gatemouth played
and played
and then
yeh
yeh

round midnight

faster than the speed of thought
no respecter of private property
but goes where it will
crasher of any party
saxaphone the high leveller
on the first set

music goes round and round
eases out the door
and comes out here
nighthawks at the diner
turning any town corner and no trees
but smoke trees
on the second set

hours pass
the world lies down to sleep
round midnight and one more ballad man
over the hills and far away
one more riff and we out ridin
on the dark road of night
on the third set

one more solo man
it's a lean reed but
one more solo man
towns like beads in the night
keep on drivin roads openin
good to the last breath
out on the night waves and don't let
silence win man or we're all
dead